START WITH A QUESTION

Can a Train Fly?

FAQs About Forces

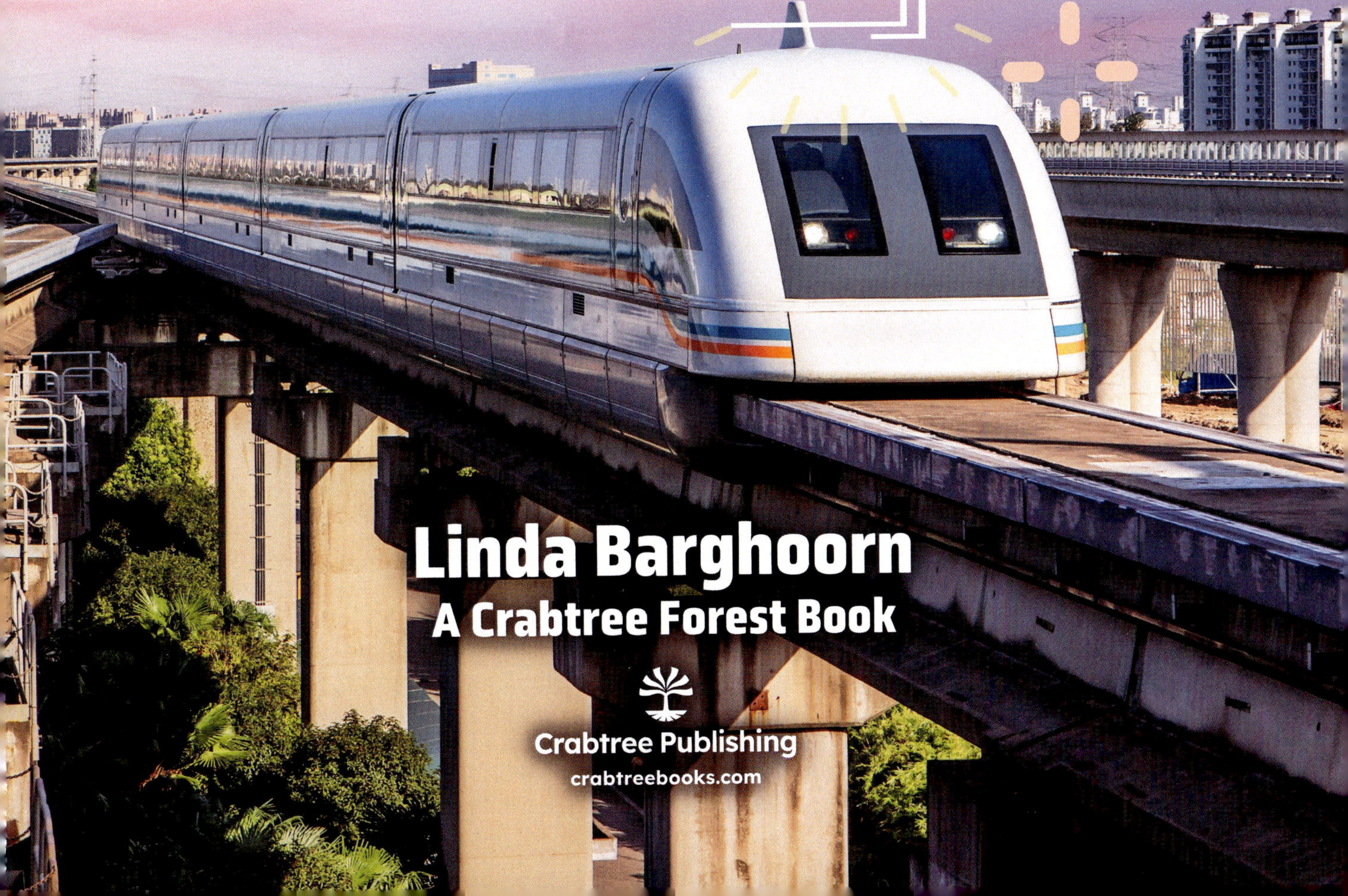

Linda Barghoorn

A Crabtree Forest Book

Crabtree Publishing
crabtreebooks.com

Notes for Readers and Class Discussion

This book is designed to teach readers about core subject areas, build curiosity, and inspire further investigation. Readers are encouraged to build upon what they already know about the subject and engage in topics they want to learn more about. Here are a few guiding questions to prompt reflection and discussion. Possible answers appear in red.

Before Reading:

Read the title and look at the table of contents. What do you already know about forces?

- *I know that there are natural forces that shape Earth, such as wind and water.*
- *I know that the force of gravity keeps us on the ground.*

What would you like to learn about forces?

- *I would like to learn how forces make the world work.*
- *I would like to learn how many different kinds of forces there are.*

During Reading:

Pause after reading each page or chapter. What questions do you have about what you read? What are you curious to know?

- *I wonder what life would be like without friction.*
- *I am curious to know how Earth's magnetic field was created.*

Make connections to what you are reading. How is this like something you already know?

- *I know that some animals migrate seasonally from colder to warmer areas.*
- *I know that wind and water shape Earth by wearing away rock over time.*

After Reading:

Recall key details about the book. What was the author trying to teach readers?

- *The author was trying to teach readers that forces affect everything people do.*
- *The author was trying to teach readers that forces can have incredible strength.*

How did the images and captions help you understand more?

- *The photographs helped me see different forces at work.*
- *The captions helped me understand more details about different kinds of forces.*

Table of Contents

Think Like a Scientist

Have you ever wondered about the forces that take place around you every day? If so, you are already thinking like a scientist. Scientists investigate topics by asking questions, carrying out experiments, and drawing conclusions. Their answers often lead to new investigations. In fact, many questions about forces are still yet to be answered!

Without forces, our lives—and our planet—would look and feel very different. Invisible forces like **gravity**, **magnetism**, and **friction** are part of almost everything we do. Earth's gravity keeps us from floating off into space, and its magnetic field protects us from the Sun's dangerous **radiation**. Friction allows us to walk and run. Forces are also at play as you plunge down the hill of a roller coaster or ride in a high-speed train!

High-speed trains travel at around 190 to 220 miles per hour (300 to 350 km/h).

The Colorado River slowly carved the Grand Canyon over millions of years.

Wind and water are also forces that shape Earth. Magnificent landscapes such as the Grand Canyon in the United States have been created over thousands of years by the incredible power of wind and water.

In this book we will explore the facts you may have wondered about forces. You may even be inspired to ask more questions and seek out new answers.

How does gravity shape our universe?

Gravity is the force that pulls objects toward the center of our planet. It prevents everything—people, buildings, and even oceans—from floating off into space. In fact, gravity holds together every piece of **matter** in our universe.

In the 17th century, an English scientist named Isaac Newton began to think about the natural forces on Earth. History claims that he watched an apple fall from a tree and wondered what made it fall down instead of up. He developed a set of ideas, which we know today as Newton's Law of Universal Gravitation. Newton stated that all objects in our universe are affected by gravity and are pulled toward each other. There is gravity between you and everything around you that has **mass**.

The force of gravity between two objects depends on their mass and distance from each other. Objects with more mass have more gravity. Objects that are close together experience more gravitational pull than objects that are far apart.

The Sun's mass is about 333,000 times the mass of Earth, so its gravitational force is always pulling our planet toward it. The speed of Earth's ***orbit*** *around the Sun, however, keeps it from being pulled into the Sun's powerful fiery sphere.*

Earth's gravitational pull is much larger than a human's. It's what makes sure we stay on the ground!

DID YOU KNOW?

The Sun makes up 99.85 percent of all the matter in our solar system. This is what makes it the most important gravitational force in our world.

Gravity played an important role in the creation of our universe billions of years ago. It was the force that pulled together swirling clouds of **atomic** dust into stars, planets, and moons.

As our solar system formed, the Sun—with its enormous mass—took center stage. Its powerful gravity pulled the planets, with their weaker gravitational forces, into its orbit. This is why our planets orbit the Sun, and not the other way around. In a similar way, moons were pulled into orbit by their more powerful planet's gravity.

The orbits of the planets and moons are also bent by gravity. Rather than being perfectly round, their orbits are elliptical, or oval-shaped. They are bent into this shape by the gravitational forces of the universe.

Black holes are unique points in space where gravity is so strong that everything around it gets pulled in. Even light cannot escape. As a result, black holes are extremely **dense**. Often these are created when a star explodes and dies, pulling all matter into its center.

Gravity created the stars and planets in our universe.

A black hole can have a mass hundreds of times greater than the Sun. That's why its gravity is so immense.

Which planets have the most gravity?

Jupiter—the largest planet in our solar system—has the strongest gravitational force. However, gravity does not only depend on an object's mass. Density also plays a role. While Jupiter's mass is more than 300 times larger than Earth's, its gravity is only twice as strong because its density is lower. This is because Jupiter is made of gases, such as hydrogen and helium, while Earth is made of dense minerals such as iron, nickel, and magnesium. Mercury, the smallest planet in our solar system, is made up almost entirely of iron. It is so dense that its gravitational force is almost one-third of Earth's—even though it is about 20 times smaller!

Jupiter and Saturn are known as gas giants. It would be impossible for a spacecraft to land on their swirling gas "surfaces."

Can gravity change our height?

Believe it or not, you are taller in the morning than you are at night. Gravity pulls down on your spine as you move around, causing you to shrink a little throughout the day. When you lie down to sleep, your spine stretches back to its full length.

Despite this, humans need gravity to be healthy. Without gravity, our bones and muscles would lose density and strength. That's because on Earth, humans are constantly using their muscles to resist gravity.

At the end of each day, you are about 0.5 inches (1.27 cm) shorter than when you got up in the morning.

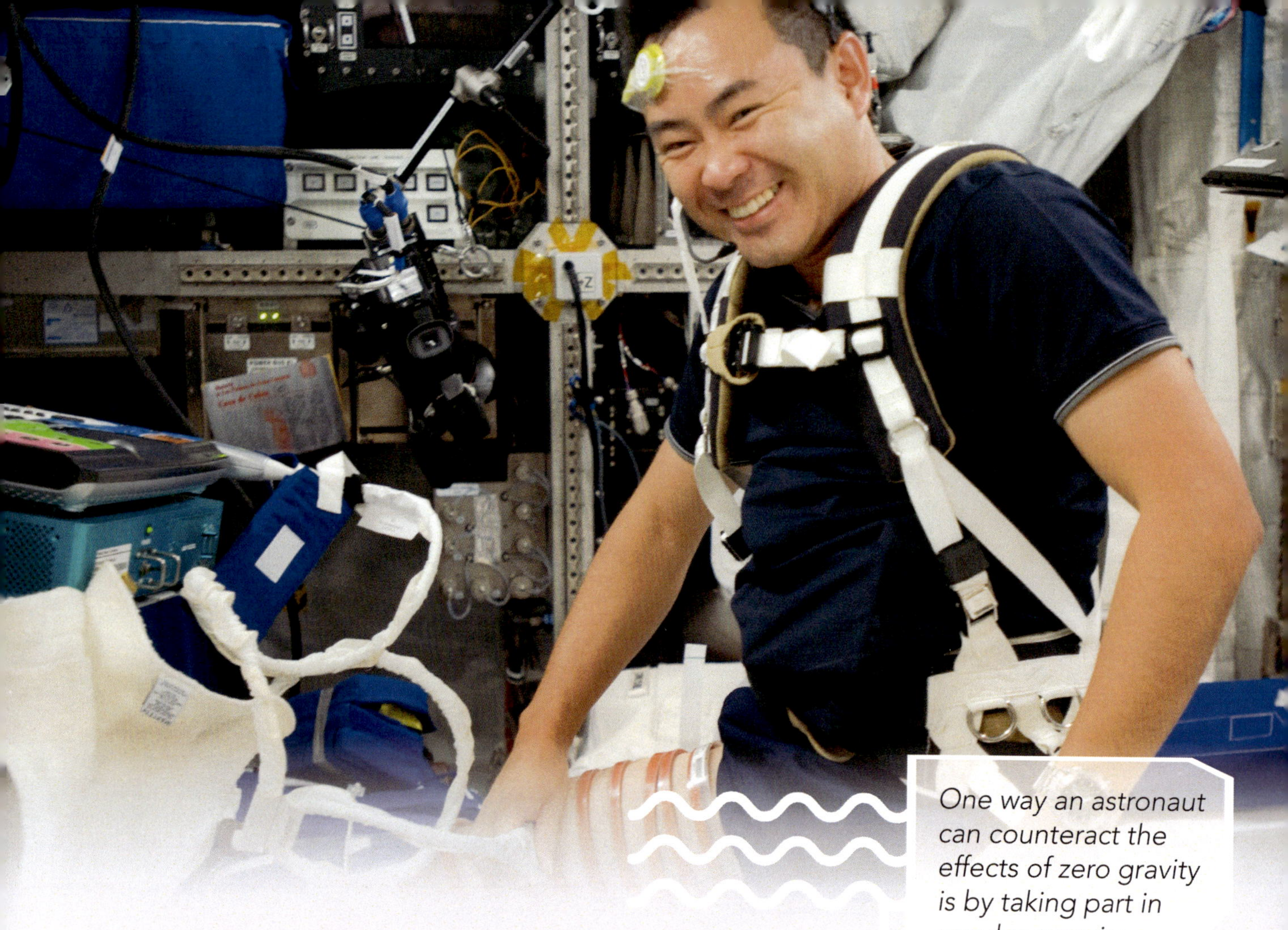

One way an astronaut can counteract the effects of zero gravity is by taking part in regular exercise.

What if there was no gravity on Earth?

Gravity is what makes planet Earth livable. Without gravity, Earth's **atmosphere** and the air we breathe would float away into space. So too would our lakes, rivers, and oceans. Without these basic elements, Earth would be unable to support any living thing.

As humans, we pay little attention to the gravity that keeps us firmly on Earth. It is a constant that we take for granted—invisible, but necessary for almost everything we do. It gives us weight, which in turn supports our skeletons and allows our bodies to move the way they do. While the idea of being weightless and able to float effortlessly might sound like fun, it would have serious effects on our bodies.

We also depend on gravity to support our modern society. It holds down the buildings, roads, and bridges that make up our cities. It keeps our cars on the road and the planes we fly in from drifting away into space. The satellites that provide us with global communication and information are held in orbit by Earth's gravity.

DID YOU KNOW?

Experts at NASA have studied the effects of zero gravity on astronauts. They learned that bones lose density in space at a rate that makes them vulnerable to breaks and fractures. Many space organizations work on strategies to minimize the effects of zero gravity on the body.

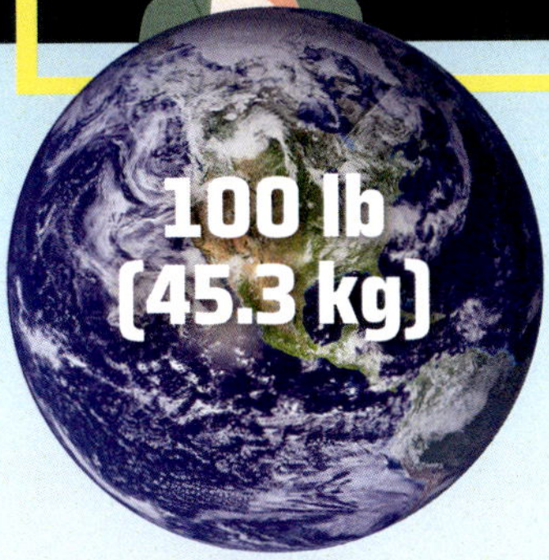

Earth

The Moon

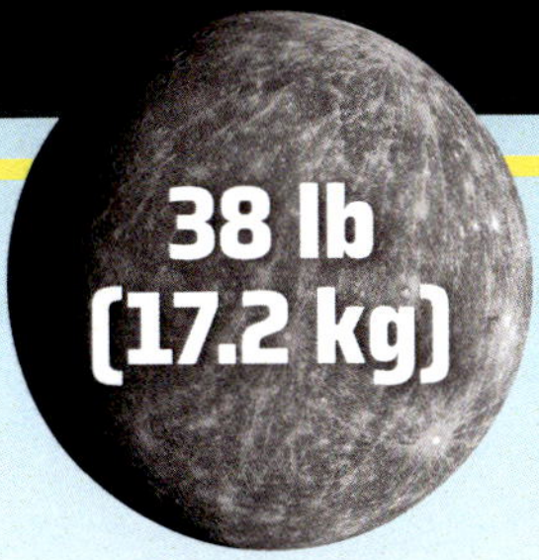

Mercury

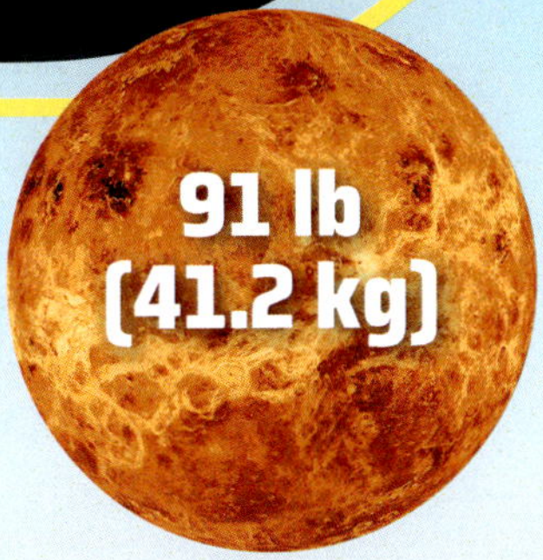

Venus

Mars

Jupiter

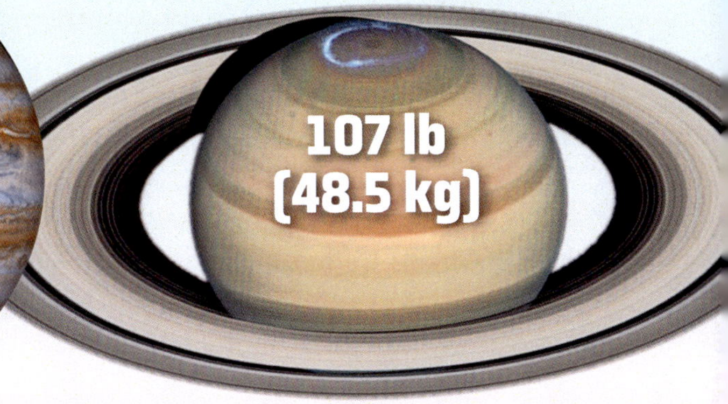

Saturn

Uranus

Earth's gravity pulls down on your body's mass, giving you weight. If you were on a planet with stronger or weaker gravity than Earth, your weight would change.

Neptune

CHAPTER 2: QUESTIONS ABOUT MAGNETISM

Why do opposites attract?

Have you ever heard the phrase "opposites attract"? Usually, we say it to suggest that people who are very different from each other can be attracted to each other. But the idea is rooted in science. It's one of the main laws, or rules, of magnetism.

Magnetism is the force through which magnets attract or repel each other. A magnet is a material or object that can produce a magnetic field that attracts certain metals, such as iron and steel. This is the area around a magnet in which the force of magnetism happens. Just like Earth, a magnet has two ends: a north pole and a south pole. Opposite poles—north and south—will attract each other. But the same poles—north and north or south and south—will push each other apart.

In fact, Earth is like a giant magnet. Its middle, or core, is made up of two metals: iron and nickel. As Earth rotates on its **axis**, its liquid metal core moves and flows as well. This movement creates a magnetic field which surrounds Earth. This magnetic field protects us from the Sun's harmful radiation.

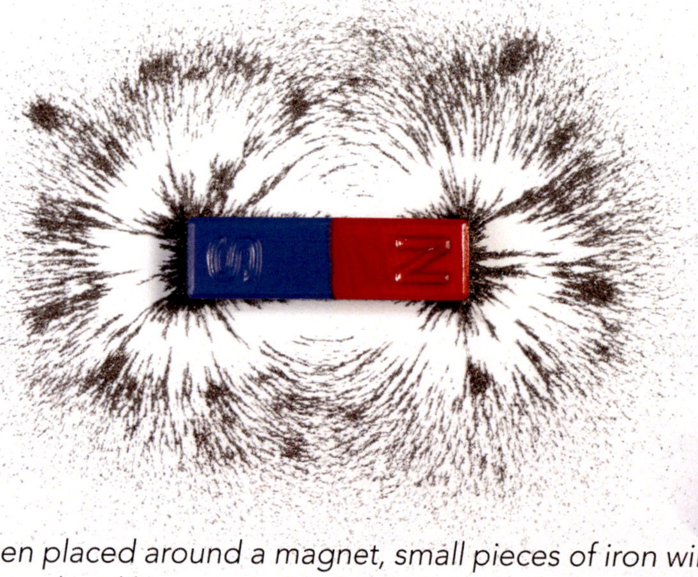

When placed around a magnet, small pieces of iron will arrange themselves like a magnetic field. That's because they have north and south poles that are attracted to or repelled by the magnet's poles.

The colorful light shows in our planet's northern night skies, known as the aurora borealis, are created when ***solar wind*** *collides with Earth's magnetic field.*

Everything on Earth is made of millions of **atoms**, which contain tiny particles called **electrons**. When these electrons spin in the same direction around the atom's core—or nucleus—they create a magnetic force. The electrons in metals like iron, cobalt, and nickel are arranged in a way that naturally makes them magnetic. Other materials, like water and wood, have very weak magnetic properties.

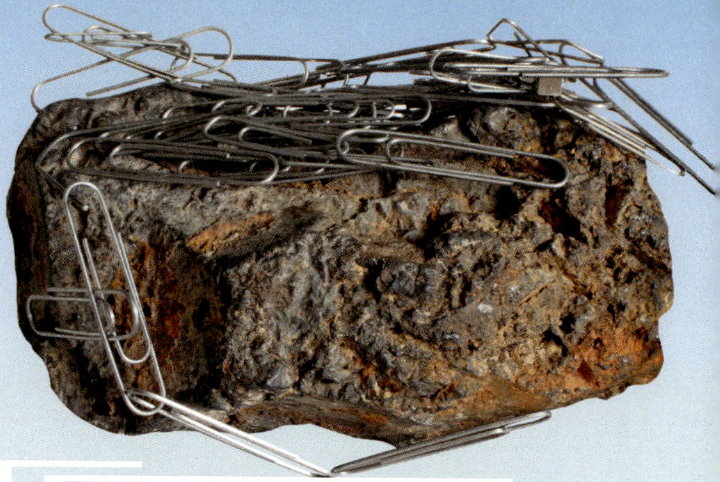

Lodestone, or magnetite (above), is the strongest naturally occurring magnet. It was used in early compasses, such as Galileo's compass (below), because it will naturally point toward Earth's North Pole.

In the 1800s, British scientist Michael Faraday discovered how to create strong human-made magnets. By wrapping a magnetic material with a coil of wire and passing an electrical **current** through it, scientists created powerful **electromagnets**.

Unlike natural magnets, electromagnets can be turned on and off by controlling the electrical supply. Powerful electromagnets can easily lift a car or truck. Today, magnets power many of the things we use in modern life—from computer hard drives to microwaves and doorbells.

DID YOU KNOW?

The strip on the back of a credit card is made of tiny magnetic particles. Each of these particles is a microscopic magnet, which stores data that is activated when you slide the card through a card reader machine.

Some large electromagnets can lift more than 13,000 pounds (5,897 kg)!

Why does a compass needle always point north?

Compasses were created to help people find their way as they explored the world. These devices imitate the behavior of Earth's North and South Poles. They have a magnetized rotating hand, which will always line up with Earth's magnetic fields. Because opposites attract, the south pole of a magnet's hand will always be attracted to Earth's North Pole. This is why a compass always points north.

DID YOU KNOW?

Earth has three "north poles." One is the geographic North Pole. This is the northern point of Earth's axis. Compasses, on the other hand, point to the magnetic North Pole. It is slightly south of the geographic North Pole. Finally, the geomagnetic North Pole is the point around which the northern lights are strongest.

The Vikings are believed to be the first people to use magnets to create compasses, which helped them cross the oceans in their quest to conquer new lands.

The magnetic and geomagnetic north poles are always moving. This is because Earth's magnetic field is always changing.

Can a train fly?

Trains have become much more modern since the first one was built in England in 1804. Though it is not possible for trains to fly, there is a type of train that can lift off the ground!

Powerful electromagnets have been used to develop high-speed trains called "maglevs" that can defy gravity. Maglev is short for "magnetic levitation." Each car, or section, in a maglev train has an extremely strong electromagnet on each of its four corners. These electromagnets create powerful magnetic fields that react with metallic loops in the train track to drive the train forward. The magnetic field is so strong that it actually causes the train to "float" about 5 inches (13 cm) above the track. This means it moves faster than trains with traditional steel wheels, which create friction on the track.

The early trains of the 1800s could travel 15 to 30 miles per hour (24 to 48 km/h). Today, high-speed maglev trains can reach 375 miles per hour (603 km/h)!

How do migratory birds know where to go?

For years, scientists have studied the **migratory** patterns of birds to understand how they are able to travel along the same routes year after year. They learned that birds use familiar landmarks and smells to help find their path.

Recent studies, however, have shown that birds might also use Earth's magnetic field to find their routes. They discovered that birds have a special **protein** called CRY4 that allows them to "see" Earth's magnetic field, which helps guide their migratory path. The angle between Earth's surface and its magnetic field provides birds with clues to help locate their migratory **breeding** sites.

The ability to see Earth's magnetic field is called magnetoreception. Studies have shown this ability in many animals, from insects to sea turtles. Some scientists are even studying this ability in humans.

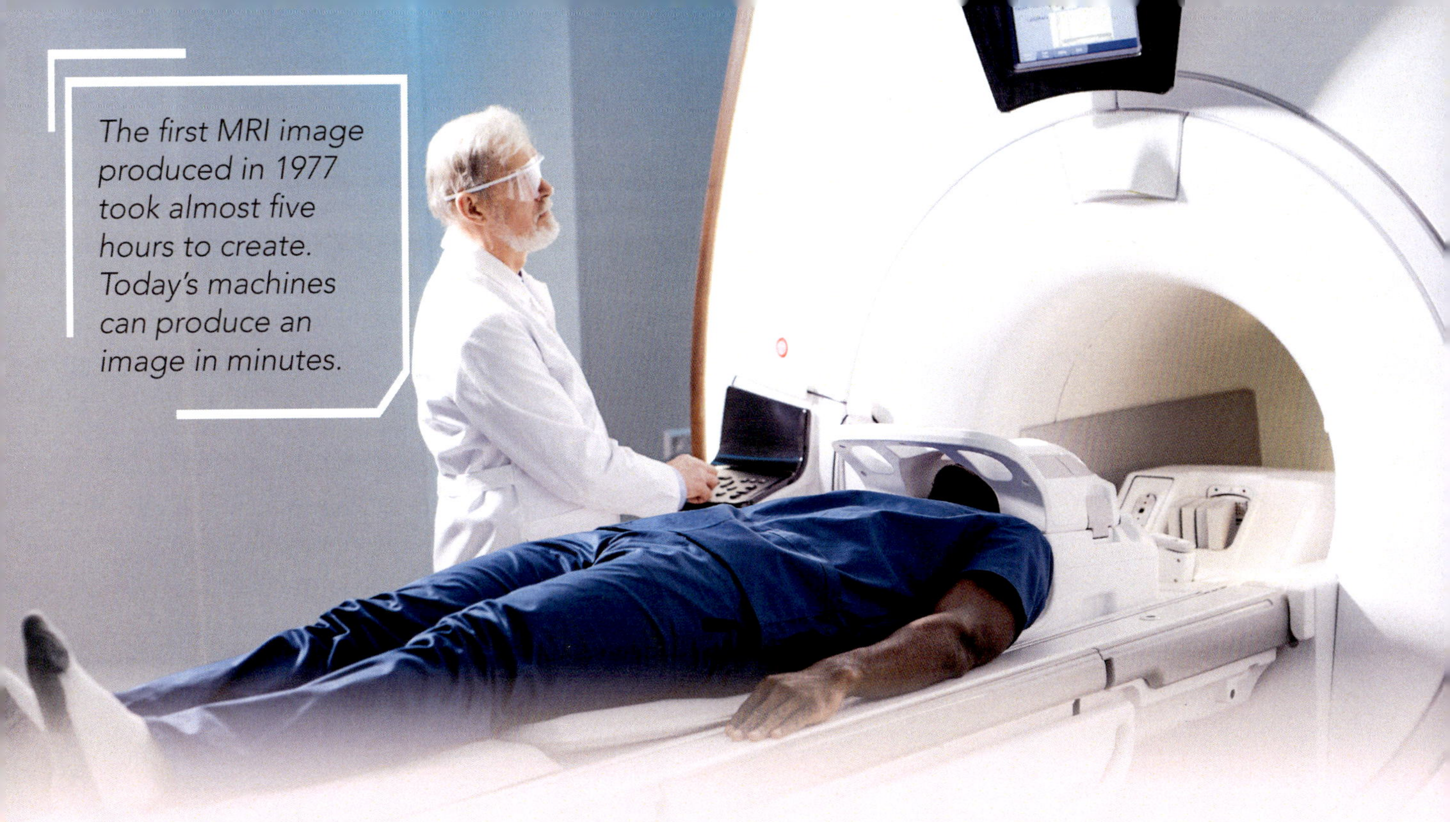

The first MRI image produced in 1977 took almost five hours to create. Today's machines can produce an image in minutes.

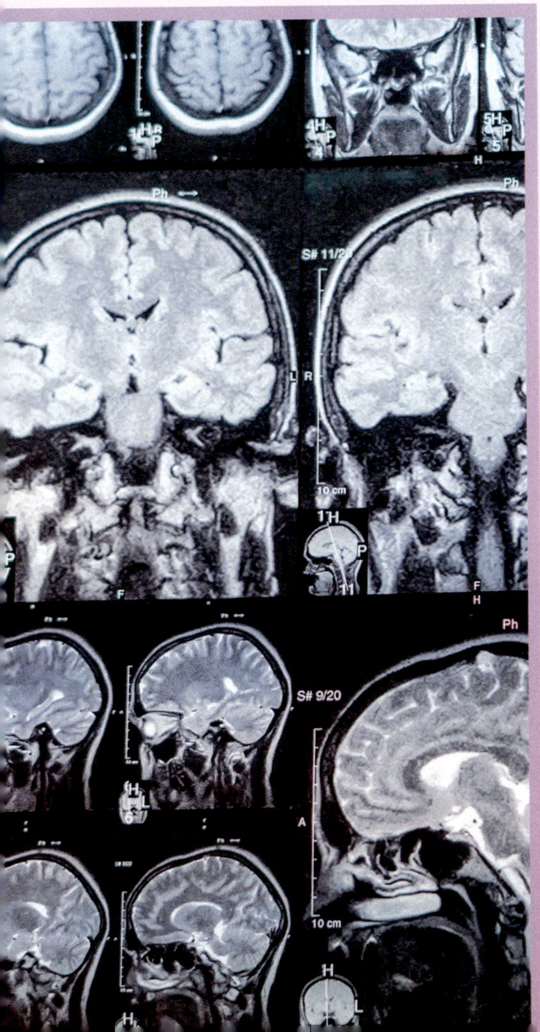

How can we see inside the human body without cutting it open?

Magnets have many uses in today's modern technologies. Some can help diagnose diseases and even save lives. Magnetic Resonance Imaging (MRI) machines provide detailed images of the human body's internal structure—from organs and muscles to bones and arteries. These machines use a magnetic field that surrounds the patient inside the machine and sends pulses of **radio waves** to scan parts of the body. These signals are converted into images that allow us to see inside the body without having to perform surgery.

How do wind and water sculpt Earth?

One of the most powerful forces on Earth is something we can't see. Wind is created by changes in Earth's atmosphere when the Sun heats different parts of the planet's surface unequally. Warm air from the **equator** rises into the atmosphere and flows toward Earth's polar regions. Cooler air moves toward the equator to replace the warm air. These air currents shape our weather and climate.

Sometimes the wind is nothing more than a pleasant, light breeze. At other times it can reach frightening speeds—in the form of hurricanes, cyclones, or tornadoes—which can be incredibly dangerous and destructive. Wind also has the power to create magnificent landscapes. By moving great quantities of sand or dust particles, wind can erode, or wear away, rock formations into weird and wonderful shapes like those found in the Altiplano desert in South America or Arches National Park in Utah, U.S.

Arches National Park

Wind created the towering sand dunes found in the Sahara desert.

Wind caused one of the largest migrations of people in American history when a series of devastating dust storms, nicknamed "black blizzards," destroyed more than 100 million acres (40 million ha) of farmland in the Great Plains region. This time in history is known as "The Dust Bowl."

Water covers almost three-quarters of Earth's surface and is key to sustaining life on our planet. Water is constantly on the move and regularly changes form—from solid to liquid to gas. As water **evaporates** from lakes and oceans it becomes water **vapor**, which forms clouds and eventually falls back to Earth as rain.

Rushing rivers wear away their riverbanks, creating valleys and canyons. The magnificent Fish River Canyon in Namibia was created by this type of erosion. Coastal erosion occurs as waves pound relentlessly on rocks, pebbles, and sand. Water currents constantly reshape islands and continents by dragging sand and pebbles away from shorelines.

Mighty glaciers are huge bodies of snow and ice formed over hundreds of thousands of years. As the size of a glacier increases, its weight is slowly pulled by gravity down a mountainside. As it slowly moves, it drags rock and sediment with it and reshapes mountain landscapes and coastlines.

Fish River Canyon is the second-largest canyon in the world after the Grand Canyon in the U.S. *(see page 26).*

DID YOU KNOW?

During the last Ice Age—between 13,000 and 25,000 years ago—much of Earth was covered with a thick layer of ice up to 2.5 miles (4 km) deep. As the ice advanced, it pushed great mounds of earth and rock, creating steep escarpments **and carving out lake beds.**

The peaks and valleys of the Lofoten Islands in Norway were eroded thousands of years ago by glaciers.

How was the Grand Canyon formed?

As a river slowly erodes its rocky riverbanks—in a process known as "downcutting"—it can create dramatic canyons or valleys. This is how the iconic Grand Canyon, in Arizona, United States, was formed.

Between 5 and 6 million years ago, the Colorado River began to wind its way across the landscape. Over millions of years its waters eroded the rocks along its banks, deepening and widening the riverbed. During winter, water trapped in cracks between the rocks froze and expanded, forcing the rocks apart and causing further erosion. Even today, erosion is still deepening and widening the Grand Canyon.

As water carved out the more than 1-mile- (1.6 km) deep canyon, it exposed layers of rock millions—and even billions—of years old.

Catamarca Province in Argentina is home to the tallest sand dune in the world—Duna Federico Kirbus, at 4,035 feet (1,230 m) tall.

Can sand dunes migrate?

Sand dunes are created when sand is blown by the wind into an obstacle, such as a plant, a rock, or a mound of earth. Heavier grains of sand settle in front of the obstacle, while lighter ones are dropped behind it. The dune grows as more and more sand is deposited. Eventually, sand at the peak of the dune will begin to slide down the other side. As it does, the sand begins to pile up on this new side and the process begins again. Over time, this causes dunes to move or "migrate."

DID YOU KNOW?

Shifting sand dunes can sing! During a large avalanche, sand particles create friction as they slide over one another. This friction creates vibrations, which can cause a humming sound.

Why does a storm howl ?

Has the wind ever seemed to howl during a storm? The noise you hear is created by friction when wind comes into contact with objects around you. As wind blows harder, the amount of friction increases and the noise becomes louder.

The sound of wind changes based on the object it encounters. As wind blows through treetops, it can make a swooshing sound. When wind is forced around solid objects, such as buildings, it splits and comes back together on the other side. As these air currents mix and encounter friction, they can make screeching or howling sounds.

A tornado, which is a powerful column of rotating winds, can cause a threatening rumbling or roaring sound, similar to that of an oncoming train.

Are some oceans higher than others?

Earth's oceans are all connected, making up one global ocean. So it may surprise you to learn that the sea level is not the same around the world. In fact, the Pacific Ocean is about 8 inches (20 cm) higher than the Atlantic Ocean. One explanation may be because the Atlantic Ocean is colder and saltier, which makes it denser and heavier than the Pacific. Ocean currents also change sea levels as they constantly move water between the oceans unevenly. Changes in the strength of Earth's gravity also affect sea levels. Where gravity is stronger, sea levels are higher.

The Panama Canal in Central America connects the Pacific and Atlantic Oceans. To get from one ocean to the other, ships must go through a system of ***locks*** *(below) that change the water level.*

CHAPTER 4: QUESTIONS ABOUT FRICTION

Is friction a good thing?

Friction is the force created by rubbing or sliding two objects together. As the surfaces meet, they "stick" to each other, causing the moving object to slow down. Friction can be created between any two states of matter.

Sometimes friction is a good thing. Metal blades on skates create friction on an icy surface, allowing you to glide instead of sticking to ice. Water helps you slide faster down a water slide. This is called fluid friction. Tires have treads that use friction to help prevent cars from skidding when driving on slippery surfaces.

It is friction that allows us to walk or run as our feet push against the ground. Without it, our feet would slip and slide backward.

Imagine a world without friction. There would be no way to stop a sliding object!

Other times, friction can cause problems. Air resistance slows an airplane down, meaning it requires more fuel to move forward. To reduce their friction with air, planes are "streamlined," or designed with smoother, curved surfaces. Friction between moving metal parts in an engine cause the machine to wear out more quickly. Oil **lubrication** is designed to reduce this friction.

The two main types of friction are static and kinetic. Static friction happens between two objects that have come into contact and have stopped moving. It's what holds something in place, such as the papers on your desk. To get an object moving, the force you apply needs to be stronger than the static friction.

Kinetic friction happens between the surfaces of moving objects. It works to bring them to a stop unless more force is applied to keep them moving. Think about moving a large rock. A lot of force may be needed to get it moving. But once the rock is in motion, it is easier to keep it going. When you stop pushing, it will come to a stop—unless it is moving downhill. In that case, the force of gravity is working to overcome friction.

The amount of friction depends on the types of surfaces involved. Dry or smooth surfaces produce less friction, while wet or rough surfaces produce more. Surfaces also interact with each other differently. You can slide across a wooden floor more easily in woolen socks than in rubber boots because there is less friction between wool and wood compared to rubber and wood.

Air resistance is also called drag. A large parachute creates enough drag to slow down the force of gravity on this skydiver.

Sliding, rolling, and fluid friction are types of kinetic friction.

Why do our hands feel warm when we rub them together?

When two surfaces are rubbed together, the tiny **molecules** on their surfaces begin to move faster. The energy created by this friction is known as frictional heat. In this process, kinetic energy is converted to thermal energy. This is what allowed early humans to create fire for warmth by rubbing sticks or flint stones together. This same process in machines, however, can cause them to overheat and become damaged. So while sometimes frictional heat can be helpful, other times it is not.

Friction welding is a way of joining two metal objects by rubbing them together at a high speed and pressure. The heat created softens the metal and fuses the objects together.

Frictional heat allows people to warm their hands by rubbing them together.

The long blades on a speed skater's skates allow the skater to glide forward at top speeds—sometimes more than 35 miles per hour (56 km/h)!

What makes ice slippery?

Ice on its own is not slippery. But add friction and watch what happens! Ice has a **crystalline structure**. Each molecule of water in each ice crystal is attached to three other molecules. But on the ice's surface, the water molecules are only attached to two other molecules. This prevents the outermost layer of ice from freezing, meaning that there is actually a thin layer of water on the ice's surface. Add friction from skate blades and this water becomes a lubricant that allows you to glide across the surface. Because different materials provide different levels of friction, a pair of rubber boots—on the other hand—will make ice slightly less slippery.

A bolt of lightning—which is a form of static electricity—carries enough energy to power a small town for a day.

Where does an electric shock come from?

Have you ever touched a doorknob and experienced a surprising shock? This is due to static electricity. Static electricity happens when an object gains an electric charge.

All objects are made up of atoms, which contain **protons**, electrons, and **neutrons**. Usually, these particles are balanced so that the atom does not have an electric charge. Friction between two materials, however, can cause electrons to jump between them and make atoms unbalanced. When you scuff your feet on carpet, your body picks up extra electrons and you gain a negative electric charge. A shock happens when you touch something that has a positive charge and the extra electrons jump from you to the new material, causing a release of energy.

Metals, such as doorknobs, have a positive charge because their atoms lose electrons easily.

How do snakes move without limbs?

Many animals depend on limbs to move around. A snake, on the other hand, has tiny hair-like structures on its scales to help it get from place to place. The structures create friction points that allow snakes to slide along the ground or even climb a tree. The structure of their scales prevents them from sliding backward when they climb.

DID YOU KNOW?

Scientists are studying the structure of snakeskin and how it uses friction for a variety of human purposes—from the tread design on sneakers to improved surface structures for artificial human joints.

Sidewinding is a type of sideways movement used only by snakes. It helps them move across loose or slippery surfaces, such as sand.

Does an object speed up as it falls?

The descent of a free-falling object—such as a skydiver jumping from a plane—is controlled by Earth's gravity. Gravity applies a force that causes an object to speed up as it falls. Each second an object falls toward Earth, it travels faster and farther than it did the second before. This is known as acceleration. But acceleration isn't simply a change in speed. It is a change in velocity, or speed in a certain direction. That means one can accelerate by changing speed or by changing the direction of movement. You can feel changes in velocity when you ride a roller coaster or when you take off in an airplane.

The higher an object is dropped from above Earth's surface, the faster it will accelerate before it hits the ground. A skydiver's free fall accelerates from the first second they jump from the plane to the last second when they touch down on the ground. Luckily, a parachute creates the drag needed to slow down this acceleration.

DID YOU KNOW?

The famous Italian scientist Galileo developed the laws of acceleration and free-falling objects in the 16th century. He determined that the force of gravity causes constant acceleration. The speed of a free-falling object increases by an equal amount within equal time periods. An apple dropped from a skyscraper, for example, has more time to accelerate before it hits the ground than an apple falling from a tree limb.

Velocity is the rate or speed at which an object is moving in a certain direction. How would you describe the velocity of this cyclist?

This four-wheeler is accelerating because it is changing direction.

Acceleration happens in three ways. You can change the speed at which you are moving. You can change the direction of your movement. Or you can change both at the same time. Positive acceleration happens when an object increases speed. Negative acceleration happens when an object is slowing down.

Speed is the measure of how quickly an object is moving. A car's speed is measured by how many miles (km) that the vehicle can travel in one hour at a certain speed. Velocity, on the other hand, measures the rate at which an object changes position, or moves in a certain direction. It depends on how far something has moved from its original position. A car that moves forward and reverses to its original position achieves zero velocity, no matter how fast it is moving.

Acceleration is a measure of how fast an object's velocity is changing. If an object's velocity is not changing, then it is not accelerating. A racecar driver can accelerate on a straightaway by speeding up or slowing down. The driver is always accelerating as the car goes into the curve of a track—even if the speed is the same—because of the change in direction.

The velocity of a racecar is measured by dividing the total distance traveled by the time it took to cover that distance.

A person moving in a circle is always accelerating, even if they do not speed up. That's because the direction of their movement is always changing.

Does a feather fall faster than a rock?

In theory, all objects, regardless of their mass, fall at the same rate of acceleration. If you dropped a feather and a rock in a vacuum—a chamber in which all the air has been removed--they would hit the ground at the same time!

In real life, however, air resistance causes the feather to fall much more slowly than the rock. The feather has more surface area relative to its mass, which creates more drag and slows its fall. The dense rock, on the other hand, can slice through the air easily.

Without air resistance, gravity causes all objects to accelerate at the same rate: 9.8 meters (32 feet) per second squared. This means that a falling object speeds up by 9.8 meters (32 feet) per second, every second.

A cheetah can accelerate from zero to 50 miles per hour (80 km/h) in just three strides. A peregrine falcon, on the other hand, can achieve diving speeds of 180 miles per hour (290 km/h).

What is Earth's fastest animal ?

The cheetah is easily Earth's fastest land animal. It is able to reach speeds of up to 68 miles per hour (109 km/h). But the cheetah isn't the fastest animal on Earth. That title belongs to the peregrine falcon, which can fly at speeds reaching 105 miles per hour (169 km/h)! Both use fast-twitch muscles, which allow them to accelerate quickly. These muscles are fueled by the animal's body to produce short bursts of energy.

How do racecars accelerate so quickly?

Racecar drivers use velocity and acceleration to achieve incredible speeds. The powerful engine of a Formula 1 (F1) car can accelerate from zero to 60 miles (97 km) in less than two seconds.

To help it travel so rapidly, a racecar has sophisticated **aerodynamic** elements, such as wings, to minimize air resistance. F1 cars also have tires with special treads that use friction to help the car stay on the track while accelerating at tremendous speed.

The record for the highest speed in an F1 race is 231.4 miles per hour (372.5 km/h). Controlled tests have even seen an F1 car reach close to 250 miles per hour (400 km/h)!

The gallop is the fastest way a horse can move. When a horse gallops, there is a point when all four of its feet are in the air!

Does the type of ground change how fast a horse can run?

Racehorses are trained on different surfaces. The type of surface they race on can determine the speed they can achieve. Some horses can achieve higher speeds on dirt tracks because dirt has less friction. But this lack of friction can also be dangerous as it is easier for the horse to slide and become injured. Grass surfaces provide more friction, which slows the horse's speed. But grass cushions the horse's stride, making it more comfortable for the horse to endure long distances safely.

Glossary

aerodynamic (air-oh-dahy-NAM-ik): Having a shape that reduces air resistance

atmosphere (AT-muhs-feer): The layers of gases surrounding a planet

atomic (uh-TOM-ik): Relating to atoms

atoms (AT-uhms): The smallest units of matter

axis (AK-sis): An imaginary line through the center of an object, around which it spins

breeding (BREE-ding): Mating and producing offspring

crystalline structure (KRIS-tl-ahyn STRUHK-cher): An arrangement of atoms in a three-dimensional, repeated pattern

current (KUR-uhnt): A steady flow of something, such as electricity, water, or air

dense (dens): Having a lot of matter packed closely together

electromagnets (ih-lek-troh-MAG-nits): Magnets created by passing an electrical current through a coil of wire

electrons (ih-LEK-trons): Parts of an atom with a negative electrical charge. Electrons surround the nucleus, or center, of an atom.

equator (ih-KWEY-ter): An imaginary line around the center of Earth, an equal distance between the North and South Poles

escarpments (ih-SKAHRP-muhnts): Steep slopes or cliffs

evaporates (ih-VAP-uh-reyts): Turns from liquid into gas

friction (FRIK-shuhn): A force that resists the movement of one object over another

gravity (GRAV-i-tee): The force that pulls objects toward Earth's center, or that pulls two objects with mass toward each other

locks (loks): Chambers or basins in canals and rivers that raise or lower boats by adding or removing water

lubrication (loo-bri-KEY-shuhn): Applying a liquid substance to a surface to reduce friction

magnetism (MAG-ni-tiz-uhm): A force that causes objects to attract or push away from each other. Magnetism happens when many electrons in an object spin in the same direction.

mass (mas): A measure of the amount of matter in an object

matter (MAT-er): Any substance that has mass and takes up space

migratory (MAHY-gruh-tawr-ee): An animal that migrates, or moves from one area to another with the seasons

molecules (MOL-uh-kyools): Groups of two or more atoms that make up the smallest units of substances

neutrons (NOO-trons): Parts of an atom with no electrical charge. Neutrons are part of an atom's nucleus.

orbit (AWR-bit): The path of one space object around another

protein (PROH-teen): A substance found in living organisms that does important work in the body's cells

protons (PROH-tons): Parts of an atom with a positive electrical charge. Protons are part of an atom's nucleus.

radiation (rey-dee-EY-shuhn): Energy that travels in waves or particles

radio waves (REY-dee-oh weyvs): A type of electromagnetic radiation often used in communication devices and in MRI

solar wind (SOH-ler wind): The constant stream of protons and electrons from the Sun's atmosphere

vapor (VEY-per): Gases or tiny drops of liquid floating in the air

Index

Comprehension Questions

1. **The Sun's mass is _______ Earth's mass.**
   a) about 300,000 times
   b) about 320,000 times
   c) about 333,000 times

2. **True or False:** Atoms contain protons, electrons, and neutrons.

3. **True or False:** Downcutting happens when a glacier slowly moves over and shapes the land.

4. **________ measures how fast an object is moving in a certain direction.**
   a) Velocity
   b) Speed
   c) Acceleration

5. **True or False:** Kinetic friction happens between the surfaces of moving objects.

6. **________ is the force that pulls objects toward the center of our planet.**
   a) Magnetism
   b) Gravity
   c) Friction

7. **True or False:** Mercury is the planet with the strongest gravity.

8. **The _______ is the point around which the northern lights are the strongest.**
   a) geographic North Pole
   b) magnetic North Pole
   c) geomagnetic North Pole

1. c, 2. True, 3. False, 4. a, 5. True, 6. b, 7. False, 8. c

About the Author

Linda Barghoorn has written 30 children's books for which she studied a wide range of topics from deserts and earthquakes to refugees, resilient cities, and remarkable people. She is an avid learner, explorer and traveler. When she's not at work, she can most often be found hiking or curled up with a good book.

Crabtree Publishing

crabtreebooks.com **800-387-7650**

In Canada: We acknowledge the financial support of the Government of Canada through the Canada Book Fund for our publishing activities.

Hardcover 978-1-0398-8092-4
Paperback 978-1-0398-8453-3
Ebook (pdf) 978-1-0398-8212-6
Epub 978-1-0398-8332-1

Printed in the U.S.A./CP2025

Published in Canada
Crabtree Publishing
616 Welland Avenue
St. Catharines, Ontario
L2M 5V6

Published in the United States
Crabtree Publishing
347 Fifth Avenue
Suite 1402-145
New York, NY 10016

Written by: Linda Barghoorn
Series development: Janine Deschenes
Editorial coordinator: Kathy Middleton
Editor: Janine Deschenes
Proofreader: Melissa Boyce
Art direction and layout: Katherine Kantor and Margaret Salter
Photo research: Katherine Kantor
Production manager: Candice Campbell

Library and Archives Canada Cataloguing in Publication
Available at the Library and Archives Canada

Library of Congress Cataloging-in-Publication Data
Available at the Library of Congress

Images:
Flickr: NASA Marshall Space Flight Center: p. 12
Shutterstock
Hasan Zaidi: p. 39 (top)
Jan van der Wolf: p. 40–41 (background)
PHOTOMDP: p. 40 (bottom left)
Wikimedia Commons
Charles Singer: p. 16 (bottom right)
All other images by Shutterstock